ELEMENTS OF
LIFE

HYDROGEN

NANCY DICKMANN

PowerKiDS
press.

Published in 2019 by **The Rosen Publishing Group, Inc.**
29 East 21st Street, New York, NY 10010

Cataloging-in-Publication Data
Names: Dickmann, Nancy.
Title: Hydrogen / Nancy Dickmann.
Description: New York : PowerKids Press, 2019. | Series: Elements of life | Includes glossary and index.
Identifiers: ISBN 9781538347614 (pbk.) | ISBN 9781538347638 (library bound) | ISBN 9781538347621 (6pack)
Subjects: LCSH: Hydrogen--Juvenile literature. | Hydrogen ions--Juvenile literature. | Chemical elements--Juvenile literature.
Classification: LCC QD181.H1 D53 2019 | DDC 546'.2--dc23

For Brown Bear Books Ltd:
Text and Editor: Nancy Dickmann
Designer and Illustrator: Supriya Sahai
Design Manager: Keith Davis
Picture Manager: Sophie Mortimer
Editorial Director: Lindsey Lowe
Children's Publisher: Anne O'Daly

Concept development: Square and Circus/Brown Bear Books Ltd

Picture Credits
Front Cover: Artwork, Supriya Sahai.
Interior: iStock: bjdizx, 15, Larisa Bozhikova, 25cr, ElenatheWise, 5, 28, Kazita Fahnizeer, 11tr, grinvalds, 9, Leonsbox, 8l, Monkey Business Images, 21, pat138241, 12, Peopleimages, 24, Sjo, 25t, vmenshov, 8br; Shutterstock: Tono Balaguer, 6–7, Jacek Chabraszewski, 14, Marcel Clemens, 10-11, 29t, Dotted Yeti, 7tr, Elena Elisseeva, 20, Everett Historical, 22-23, 29b, Outer Space, 19t, solarsevan, 19br.
Key: t=top, b=bottom, c=center, l=left, r=right

Brown Bear Books have made every attempt to contact the copyright holders. If you have any information please contact licensing@brownbearbooks.co.uk

Manufactured in the United States of America

CPSIA Compliance Information: Batch CWPK19: For Further Information contact Rosen Publishing, New York, New York at 1-800-237-9932

CONTENTS

ELEMENTS ALL AROUND US

Elements are everywhere! They make up everything in the universe, from guppies to galaxies. Elements cannot be broken down into other substances. Oxygen, carbon, hydrogen, nitrogen, phosphorus, and sulfur are the most important elements for life.

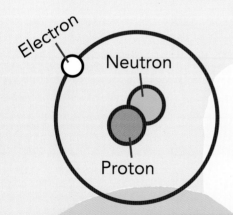

Electron
Neutron
Proton

ATOMS AND MOLECULES

Each element is made up of countless smaller, identical parts. These tiny particles, called atoms, are made up of even smaller particles. Neutrons and protons are in the nucleus at the center of the atom. Electrons circle around the nucleus. Atoms of different elements can bond together, forming a compound. The compound might look and react very differently from the original elements.

THE HYDROGEN ATOM

A hydrogen atom has 1 electron and 1 proton. Nearly all have 1 neutron, but a few have 2 or none.

HYDROGEN EVERYWHERE

There are more atoms of hydrogen in the universe than any other element. On Earth, most hydrogen is found in compounds. Water is a hydrogen compound, and so are many rocks and minerals.

Hydrogen and oxygen are both gases. When they combine, they form a very important liquid: water.

Natural or Not?

There are about 94 elements that are found in nature. Others have been made in laboratories.

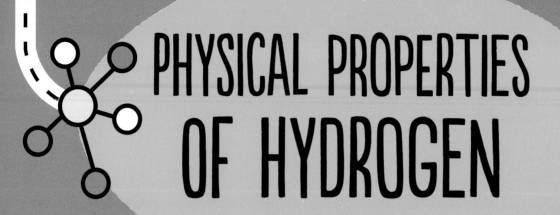

PHYSICAL PROPERTIES OF HYDROGEN

Every element has its own unique characteristics. Some of them can be easily measured without changing the element into another substance. They are called physical properties.

LOCKED UP

Physical properties describe an element in its pure state. But on Earth, it is rare to find hydrogen on its own. Water and other compounds containing hydrogen have different physical properties than hydrogen on its own.

All of Earth's water contains hydrogen. There may also be free hydrogen beneath the ocean floor.

LOOKING AT HYDROGEN

Even if you had a quantity of pure hydrogen, you wouldn't be able to see or touch it. But this still tells you something about its physical properties. An element's color and odor are physical properties.

The planet Jupiter is made mainly of hydrogen.

STATE: Hydrogen is a gas at room temperature. It only condenses to a liquid form at a very low temperature of –423.18°F (–252.88°C).

COLOR: Hydrogen is colorless and transparent, meaning see-through.

ODOR: Hydrogen has no odor or taste.

DENSITY: Hydrogen is the least dense of all the elements.

CHEMICAL PROPERTIES OF HYDROGEN

An element's chemical properties are different from its physical properties. They can only be observed when it reacts with other elements or substances.

CHEMICAL CHANGES

Some elements, like hydrogen, easily combine with other elements. The atoms of each element are rearranged to form new substances. This is called a chemical change. An element's chemical properties can be measured when this happens.

The citric acid in lemons and oranges is a compound that contains hydrogen.

Hydrogen reacts with carbon and oxygen to form compounds called hydrocarbons, found in the gasoline that fuels our cars.

PHYSICAL OR CHEMICAL?

When a shredder cuts a sheet of paper into thin strips, that is a physical change. The paper is still paper, and you could tape it back together. But if you burn the paper, that is a chemical change. New substances, such as ash, are formed. You cannot turn the ash back into paper.

ALL ABOUT HYDROGEN

Here are a few of hydrogen's chemical properties:

Hydrogen can burn in the presence of oxygen. This reaction produces water.

Hydrogen is very reactive. It reacts with many other elements.

Hydrogen is very explosive. When mixed with air and exposed to a spark, it will explode.

In its pure form hydrogen tends to form molecules, each made up of two hydrogen atoms.

WHERE IS HYDROGEN FOUND?

With just one proton, hydrogen is the simplest element. It's also the most common—more than 90 percent of all the atoms in the universe are hydrogen!

FREE HYDROGEN

There are tiny amounts of free hydrogen in the atmosphere. But hydrogen is so light that much of it escapes into space. Scientists have found pockets of hydrogen underground. But most of the hydrogen on Earth is joined with other elements in compounds.

Hydrogen gets its name from Greek words meaning "water forming."

WATER WORLD

Earth is called the "blue planet" thanks to its oceans. Water is everywhere: in rivers and lakes, in glaciers, and even in the air. Each molecule of water has two hydrogen atoms and one oxygen atom, giving it a chemical formula of H_2O.

Many minerals, including talc, contain hydrogen.

IN THE CRUST

By weight, hydrogen makes up about 0.14 percent of Earth's crust. It is joined with other elements inside minerals.

HOW HYDROGEN WAS DISCOVERED

In 1766, the English chemist Henry Cavendish added iron filings to sulfuric acid. He was able to prove that the bubbles this produced were different from other gases. He called it "inflammable air." In 1781, he discovered that hydrogen produces water when it is burned.

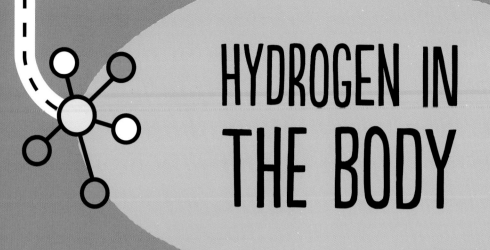

HYDROGEN IN THE BODY

Did you know that about 60 percent of your body mass is made up of water? Every day, you drink more. All that water means a lot of hydrogen!

THE BIG FOUR

Just four elements make up about 96 percent of the human body: oxygen, carbon, hydrogen, and nitrogen. Hydrogen makes up about 10 percent of your body's mass. There are actually more atoms of hydrogen in the body than any other element. But they are so light that they make up a fairly small percentage of the overall mass.

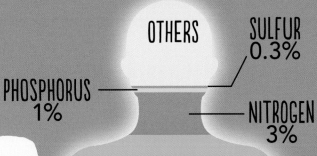

OTHERS

SULFUR
0.3%

PHOSPHORUS
1%

NITROGEN
3%

HYDROGEN
10%

CARBON
18%

OXYGEN
65%

WATER

Most of the body's hydrogen is found in water. Water is incredibly important to the body.

Water acts as a shock absorber for the brain and spinal cord.

Water is a main component of blood, which carries oxygen and nutrients to all parts of the body.

Water is a component of most body parts—even bones!

Sweat is mainly water. Sweating helps cool the body down when it gets too hot.

As urine, water plays an important role in flushing waste out of the body.

OTHER COMPOUNDS

Carbohydrates, lipids, and proteins all contain hydrogen. These nutrients are all found in the food we eat, and they are crucial for life.

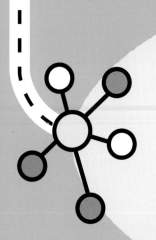

HYDROGEN AND LIFE

Plants and animals are made up of organic compounds. These substances contain carbon, which is bonded to other elements—usually including hydrogen.

The "fiber" in vegetables and whole grains is actually cellulose. It helps keep your digestive system healthy.

BUILDING BLOCKS

Organic compounds are crucial for life. Proteins are the building blocks of the body, forming tissues and organs. Lipids provide insulation and energy. Carbohydrates provide fuel for the body. Sugars and starches are carbohydrates. So is cellulose, which forms the cell walls of green plants.

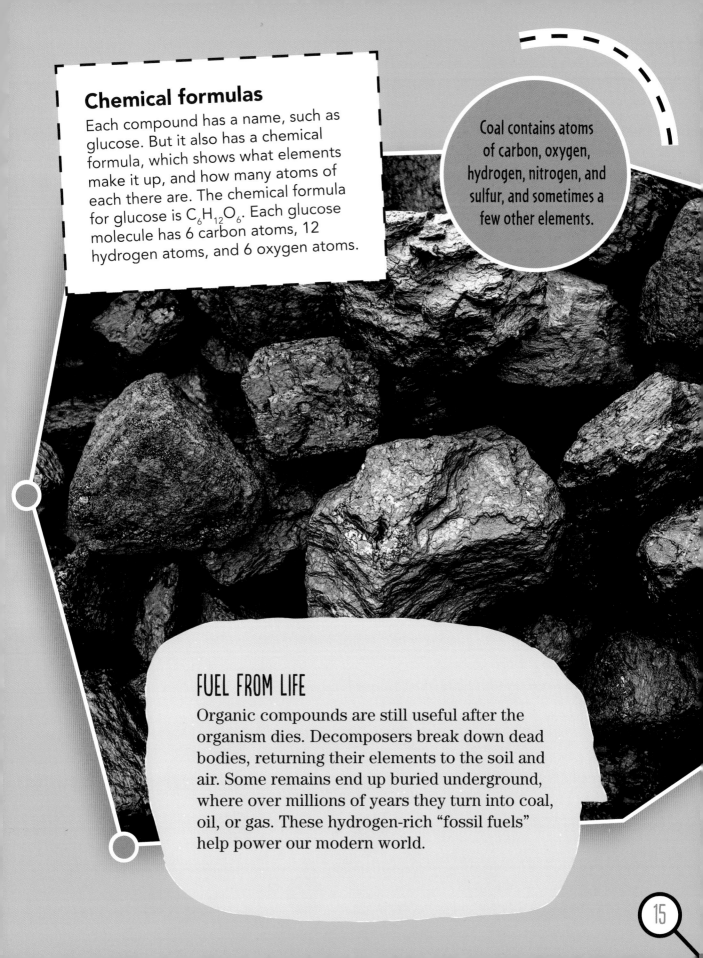

Chemical formulas

Each compound has a name, such as glucose. But it also has a chemical formula, which shows what elements make it up, and how many atoms of each there are. The chemical formula for glucose is $C_6H_{12}O_6$. Each glucose molecule has 6 carbon atoms, 12 hydrogen atoms, and 6 oxygen atoms.

Coal contains atoms of carbon, oxygen, hydrogen, nitrogen, and sulfur, and sometimes a few other elements.

FUEL FROM LIFE

Organic compounds are still useful after the organism dies. Decomposers break down dead bodies, returning their elements to the soil and air. Some remains end up buried underground, where over millions of years they turn into coal, oil, or gas. These hydrogen-rich "fossil fuels" help power our modern world.

WE NEED WATER

Hydrogen's role as a component of water is incredibly important. Without water, there would be no life on Earth.

HYDROGEN BONDS

In a water molecule, the one oxygen and two hydrogen atoms form a V shape. There is a positive electrical charge near the hydrogen atoms, and at the oxygen end there is a negative charge. Positive charges are naturally attracted to negative ones, so water molecules tend to stick to each other.

Water vapor cools slightly and forms clouds.

Water evaporates (turns into a gas) and rises into the air.

The negative charge of the oxygen end is attracted to the positive charge of the hydrogen end of another water molecule.

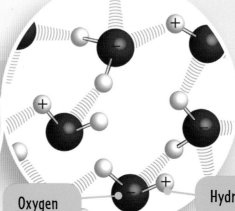

Oxygen

Hydrogen

THE WATER CYCLE

Water on Earth is recycled again and again. It moves through the air, water, and land—and even the bodies of living things!

Water falls from clouds onto the ground in the form of rain, hail, or snow.

Plants take in water from the ground through their roots. They release water vapor through their leaves.

Animals drink water. They breathe out water vapor.

Some water seeps into the ground.

Some water collects in rivers and travels back to the ocean.

STAR MAKER

Hydrogen forms bright stars, including our own sun. It is the fuel that allows them to shine. Without hydrogen, our planet would be too dark and cold for life.

INSIDE A STAR

Deep inside a star, it is incredibly hot. There is intense, crushing pressure. These conditions are perfect for a nuclear reaction called fusion. Atoms of hydrogen fuse together. They form an element called helium. This process releases energy.

Chemical or nuclear?

Fusion is a nuclear reaction. The number of protons inside the nuclei changes. This makes a different element. A chemical reaction is different. The atoms' electrons are rearranged, but the nuclei stay the same.

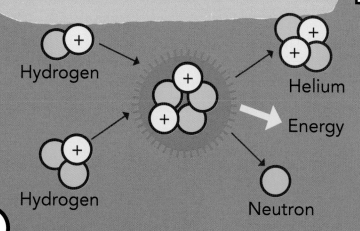

Hydrogen

Hydrogen

Helium

Energy

Neutron

Two hydrogen atoms smash into each other. Their nuclei fuse, forming an atom of helium. Energy is released, along with a spare neutron.

HYDROGEN EVERYWHERE

Hydrogen is not just found in stars. Large gas planets, like Jupiter and Saturn, are found throughout the universe. They are mostly made of hydrogen. There is also hydrogen in the huge clouds of gas and dust in space.

The energy released by nuclear fusion in the sun reaches us as heat and light.

ALL ABOUT ACIDS

Hydrogen forms a key part of compounds called acids. These have special properties and are very useful.

SPLITTING UP

When water is added to an acid, the acid's molecules split apart and release hydrogen ions. (A hydrogen ion is a proton with a positive charge.) The opposite of an acid is a base. When added to water, a base will split apart and release a different kind of ion, with a negative charge.

Measuring Up

Acids and bases are measured on a scale called the pH scale. This scale goes from 0 to 14. The more acidic a substance is, the lower the number. Pure water is 7: right in the middle. It is neither an acid or a base.

Some vegetables contain an acid called folic acid. It helps keep our blood healthy.

ACIDS IN NATURE

Acids taste sour, and they can eat away at other materials. Lemon juice and vinegar are both acids. There are acids in your stomach, which help break down food. One of the most important acids is DNA. This complicated molecule is found in every cell. It carries instructions that control traits, such as the color of your eyes or the shape of your nose.

DNA is passed from parent to child. That is why you look like your parents!

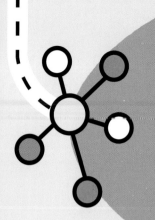

LIGHTER THAN AIR

Hydrogen is the lightest element. It is lighter than air, a property that has made it very useful.

WHAT IS AIR?

The air that we breathe is a mixture of different gases. The main two are nitrogen and oxygen. There are also small amounts of argon, carbon dioxide, and other gases. A nitrogen atom has 7 protons and an oxygen atom has 8. Hydrogen atoms, with just a single proton, easily float above these other gases.

Isotopes

Most elements have several forms, called isotopes. Isotopes have the same number of protons and electrons, but a different number of neutrons. Hydrogen has three main isotopes, each with its own special name. Tritium has two neutrons and deuterium has one. Protium, the most common type of hydrogen, has no neutrons.

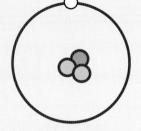

Tritium

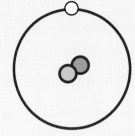

Deuterium

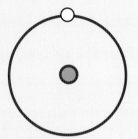

Protium

Nearly all hydrogen on Earth is protium.

A hydrogen airship could take passengers from Europe to the United States in just a few days—faster than a boat.

AIRSHIPS

Scientists have known for hundreds of years that hydrogen is lighter than air. In 1785, a French inventor used a hydrogen-filled balloon to fly across the English Channel. In the early 1900s, before there were passenger jets, huge hydrogen airships carried people across the Atlantic Ocean.

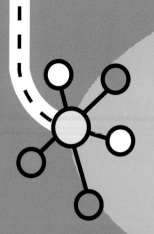

USING HYDROGEN

Although pure hydrogen is rare on Earth, it is extremely useful. Scientists produce hydrogen for a variety of uses.

Hydrogen is used in the production of the silicon chips at the heart of many electronic devices.

In a fuel cell, hydrogen "fuel" is mixed with oxygen to produce electricity. The only waste product is water, so it is a clean fuel. Some cars and buses already run on hydrogen fuel cells.

In glassmaking, hydrogen is used to help produce large, flat plates of crystal-clear glass. The molten glass "floats" on molten tin, and the hydrogen keeps the tin from reacting with oxygen in the air—which could cause flaws in the glass.

Hydrogen can be added to turn liquid vegetable oils into semi-solid fats, such as margarine.

WHERE DOES IT COME FROM?

There is hydrogen in natural gas, and it can be isolated by heating natural gas with steam. This forms a mixture of hydrogen and carbon monoxide, which can be separated. It is also possible to produce hydrogen by using electricity to split water molecules apart.

Hydrogen is used in factories to produce ammonia, a key ingredient in fertilizers, dyes, nylon, and some cleaning products.

THE PERIODIC TABLE

All the elements are organized into a chart called the periodic table. It groups together elements with similar properties. Each square gives information about a particular element.

A Good Idea!

The periodic table was developed in the 1860s by a Russian chemist named Dmitri Mendeleev. He left gaps that were later filled in with new elements, as they were discovered.

The columns are called groups. Elements in a group have similar properties.

The rows are called periods. Reading from left to right, the atomic numbers of the elements go up, from 1 to 118.

Period / **Group**

	1	2	3	4	5	6	7	8
1	1 **H** Hydrogen 1.008							
2	3 **Li** Lithium 6.94	4 **Be** Beryllium 9.0122						
3	11 **Na** Sodium 22.990	12 **Mg** Magnesium 24.305						
4	19 **K** Potassium 39.098	20 **Ca** Calcium 40.078	21 **Sc** Scandium 44.956	22 **Ti** Titanium 47.867	23 **V** Vanadium 50.942	24 **Cr** Chromium 51.996	25 **Mn** Manganese 54.938	26 **Fe** Iron 55.845
5	37 **Rb** Rubidium 85.468	38 **Sr** Strontium 87.62	39 **Y** Yttrium 88.906	40 **Zr** Zirconium 91.224	41 **Nb** Niobium 92.906	42 **Mo** Molybdenum 95.95	43 **Tc** Technetium	44 **Ru** Ruthenium 101.07
6	55 **Cs** Cesium 132.91	56 **Ba** Barium 137.33	57–71	72 **Hf** Hafnium 178.49	73 **Ta** Tantalum 180.95	74 **W** Tungsten 183.84	75 **Re** Rhenium 186.21	76 **Os** Osmium 190.23
7	87 **Fr** Francium	88 **Ra** Radium	89–103	104 **Rf** Rutherfordium	105 **Db** Dubnium	106 **Sg** Seaborgium	107 **Bh** Bohrium	108 **Hs** Hassium

57 **La** Lanthanum 138.91	58 **Ce** Cerium 140.12	59 **Pr** Praseodymium 140.91	60 **Nd** Neodymium 144.24	61 **Pm** Promethium	62 **Sm** Samarium 150.36
89 **Ac** Actinium	90 **Th** Thorium 232.04	91 **Pa** Protactinium 231.04	92 **U** Uranium 238.03	93 **Np** Neptunium	94 **Pu** Plutonium

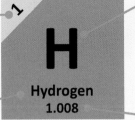

1

H
Hydrogen
1.008

| 9 | 10 | 11 | 12 | 13 | 14 | 15 | 16 | 17 | 18 |

Metalloids (semimetals)

Non–metals

Metals

									2 He Helium 4.0026
				5 B Boron 10.81	6 C Carbon 12.011	7 N Nitrogen 14.007	8 O Oxygen 15.999	9 F Fluorine 18.998	10 Ne Neon 20.180
				13 Al Aluminum 26.982	14 Si Silicon 28.085	15 P Phosphorus 30.974	16 S Sulfur 32.06	17 Cl Chlorine 35.45	18 Ar Argon 39.948
27 Co Cobalt 58.933	28 Ni Nickel 58.693	29 Cu Copper 63.546	30 Zn Zinc 65.38	31 Ga Gallium 69.723	32 Ge Germanium 72.630	33 As Arsenic 74.922	34 Se Selenium 78.971	35 Br Bromine 79.904	36 Kr Krypton 83.798
45 Rh Rhodium 102.91	46 Pd Palladium 106.42	47 Ag Silver 107.87	48 Cd Cadmium 112.41	49 In Indium 114.82	50 Sn Tin 118.71	51 Sb Antimony 121.76	52 Te Tellurium 127.60	53 I Iodine 126.90	54 Xe Xenon 131.29
77 Ir Iridium 192.22	78 Pt Platinum 195.08	79 Au Gold 196.97	80 Hg Mercury 200.59	81 Tl Thallium 204.38	82 Pb Lead 207.2	83 Bi Bismuth 208.98	84 Po Polonium	85 At Astatine	86 Rn Radon
109 Mt Meitnerium	110 Ds Darmstadtium	111 Rg Roentgenium	112 Cn Copernicium	113 Nh Nihonium	114 Fl Flerovium	115 Mc Moscovium	116 Lv Livermorium	117 Ts Tennessine	118 Og Oganesson

63 Eu Europium 151.96	64 Gd Gadolinium 157.25	65 Tb Terbium 158.93	66 Dy Dysprosium 162.50	67 Ho Holmium 164.93	68 Er Erbium 167.26	69 Tm Thulium 168.93	70 Yb Ytterbium 173.05	71 Lu Lutetium 174.97

Lanthanide elements

95 Am Americium	96 Cm Curium	97 Bk Berkelium	98 Cf Californium	99 Es Einsteinium	100 Fm Fermium	101 Md Mendelevium	102 No Nobelium	103 Lr Lawrencium

Actinide elements

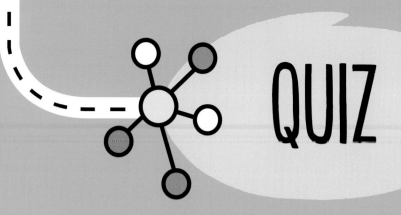

QUIZ

Try this quiz and test your knowledge of hydrogen and elements! The answers are on page 32.

1

What are atoms made of?

a. elements and compounds
b. sugar and spice
c. protons, neutrons, and electrons

2

What happens to most free hydrogen in the atmosphere?

a. it escapes into space
b. it freezes and falls as snow
c. it mixes with sunlight and turns into gold

3

What will happen if you mix hydrogen with air and introduce a spark?

a. it will turn into water
b. it will explode
c. nothing

5

How much of your body is made up of water?

a. just the blood, sweat, and tears
b. about 60 percent
c. everything except hair and bones

4

Why is there so little free hydrogen on Earth?

a. it disappeared when an asteroid crashed into Earth
b. nothing is free anymore, not even hydrogen
c. it very easily forms bonds with other elements

7

What process takes place inside a star?

a. nuclear fission
b. nuclear fusion
c. nuclear family

6

What happens in the water cycle?

a. water is recycled between the air, the ground, and the oceans
b. laundry detergent is rinsed away
c. the body takes in water and gets rid of urine

8

Why was hydrogen used in airships?

a. it was ideal for keeping the engines clean
b. it was cheaper than jet fuel
c. it is lighter than air

GLOSSARY

acid a substance with a low pH that usually has a sour taste and eats away other materials

atmosphere the layers of gases that surround the earth

atom the smallest possible unit of a chemical element

base a substance with a high pH; the opposite of an acid

bond to form a link with other atoms of the same element or of a different element

carbohydrates compounds such as sugars and starches, which are made from carbon, hydrogen, and oxygen

carbon dioxide gas found in the air that plants need to survive

cell the smallest unit of life. All plants and animals are made of cells.

chemical change change that occurs when one substance reacts with another to form a new substance

chemical property characteristic of a material that can be observed during or after a chemical reaction

compound substance made of two or more different elements bonded together

crust the hard, outermost layer of Earth

decomposer small living thing that breaks down dead matter

electron a tiny particle of an atom with a negative charge

element a substance that cannot be broken down or separated into other substances

energy the ability to do work. Energy can take many forms.

evaporate to turn from a liquid into a gas

fuel anything that can be burned as a source of energy, such as wood or gasoline

fusion nuclear reaction in which nuclei fuse together to form a new element

gas matter that is neither liquid or solid

hydrocarbons compounds made up of carbon and hydrogen atoms, which occur in oil, coal, and gas

isotopes different forms of the same element. Isotopes of an element have different numbers of neutrons.

liquid matter that is neither solid nor gas, and flows when it is poured

mass the total amount of matter in an object or space

molecule the smallest unit of a substance that has all the properties of that substance. A molecule can be made up of a single atom, or a group of atoms

neutron a particle in the nucleus of an atom

nucleus the center of an atom

organic compound chemical compound that includes carbon atoms bonded to other elements

physical property characteristic of a material that can be observed without changing the material

proton a positively charged particle in the nucleus of an atom

react to undergo a chemical change when combined with another substance

FURTHER RESOURCES

BOOKS

Arbuthnott, Gill. *Your Guide to the Periodic Table.* New York, NY: Crabtree Publishing Company, 2016.

Callery, Sean, and Miranda Smith. *Periodic Table.* New York, NY: Scholastic Nonfiction, 2017.

Gifford, Clive. *Stars, Galaxies, and the Milky Way.* New York, NY: Crabtree Publishing Company, 2016.

MacCarald, Clara. *Hydrogen.* New York, NY: Enslow Publishing, 2018.

Marquardt, Meg. *Hydrogen Fuel Cells.* Minneapolis, MN: Core Library, 2017.

Stewart, Melissa. *Water.* Washington, DC: National Geographic, 2014.

WEBSITES

This website has facts about acids and bases:
www.chem4kids.com/files/react_acidbase.html

Go here for amazing facts about hydrogen:
www.ducksters.com/science/chemistry/hydrogen.php

Learn about all the elements using this interactive periodic table:
www.rsc.org/periodic-table/

Learn more about the water in your body:
water.usgs.gov/edu/propertyyou.html

Publisher's note to educators and parents: Our editors have carefully reviewed these websites to ensure that they are suitable for students. Many websites change frequently, however, and we cannot guarantee that a site's future contents will continue to meet our high standards of quality and educational value. Be advised that students should be closely supervised whenever they access the Internet.

INDEX

Quiz answers
1. c; 2. a; 3. b; 4. c; 5. b;
6. a; 7. b; 8. c